Looking at Minibeasts

Spiders, Centipedes, and Millipedes

Sally Morgan

Thameside Press

Contents

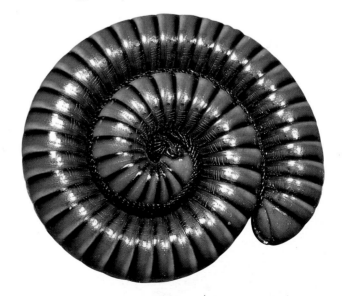

Words in **bold** are
explained on page 31.

What is a spider?

Spiders have eight long legs and eight eyes.
They have strong jaws. A spider's body is
made up of two parts—a head at the front
and an **abdomen**
at the back.

The tarantula has
a large body which
is covered in hairs.

This spider has two large eyes on the front of its head. The other six eyes look sideways and backward.

Spiders can be all shapes and sizes. The largest is the bird-eating spider. It lives in rain forests, and can grow to the size of a dinner plate. All spiders use their long legs to run quickly across the ground.

The money spider is one of the smallest spiders.

The spider family

Spiders belong to a group of animals called **arachnids**. They are not **insects**. Scorpions, ticks, and mites are arachnids too. The scorpion has a long tail with a **sting** at the end. It has a large pair of powerful claws to grip its **prey**.

The scorpion holds its tail over its body, ready to use its sting.

Mites have eight legs and a large body.

Mites and

ticks are tiny animals

that live on other creatures. They bite through

the skin of the animal on which they live, and

feed by sucking the

animal's blood.

This tick is living on the body of an animal called a tapir.

Colors and shapes

Many of the spiders we see every day are a plain brown color. Some tropical spiders are brightly colored. The calico spider has a body which is colored orange and black.

This calico spider is waiting for prey in the middle of its web.

This tarantula is red and black to warn other animals that it has a painful bite.

Some spiders have bright green, **armored** bodies. Others have heavy, hairy bodies and short legs. The harvestman spider has a small body and very long legs.

You can barely see the long, thin legs of this harvestman spider.

Centipedes and millipedes

Centipedes (above) and millipedes have long, thin bodies with many pairs of legs. Their bodies are protected by a tough covering which is a bit like armor.

The giant millipede is covered in shiny black and orange armor.

This covering cannot stretch. As the animal grows, it has to **shed** its covering from time to time. The bodies of centipedes and millipedes are made up of many parts called **segments**.

Millipedes have two eyes, two feelers, and powerful jaws.

Hundreds of legs

The word millipede means 1,000 legs. Millipedes

have lots of legs, but they do not have 1,000!

The largest millipedes have several hundred legs.

Some tropical millipedes have bright-red legs.

There are two pairs of legs on each segment.

The red legs of a giant millipede look like a fringe sticking out from beneath its armored body.

The word centipede means 100 legs, but centipedes can have between 34 and 250 legs. They have two legs attached to each segment of their bodies—one leg on each side.

This centipede has a pair of legs on each segment of its body.

Fast and slow

Spiders can run quickly on their eight legs. Their sudden movements scare some people. Each leg is made up of several sections, which are joined together. A spider can bend each leg at these **joints**.

Millipedes cannot move quickly. They crawl along with slow, wavy movements.

In real life, an African millipede is as long as this picture.

The wolf spider is a hunter. It uses its long legs to chase other animals.

Centipedes move faster than millipedes because they have to catch their prey.

A jumping spider (above) leaps onto its prey from a distance.

Spinning webs

Many spiders spin a web to catch their food.

The web is made from very strong threads

of **silk**. Some of the threads are sticky.

A spider's web is made from silk threads. Some spiders spin a new web every day.

This spider is pushing out silk from the back of its abdomen.

The spider waits in the middle of its web. An insect which flies into the web gets trapped on the sticky threads. The web moves as the insect struggles to escape. This tells the spider that dinner is ready! A spider can catch as many as 100 insects in its web every day.

A spider wraps up an insect in a bundle of silk, and then leaves the insect until it is hungry.

Web styles

There are many different types of spider's webs. The garden spider spins a large spiral web. Some spiders spin a web that looks like a sheet on the ground. It's ideal for catching insects that crawl and hop. A water spider traps air in its web, and then breathes the air when it is underwater.

The web-casting spider makes a small, sticky web to throw over its prey.

A jumping spider sits in the middle of its web, waiting for prey.

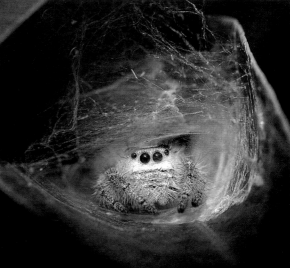

Hunting for food

Spiders and centipedes are hunting animals. They are called **carnivores**. This means that they feed on other animals. Not all spiders spin webs to catch their prey. The trapdoor spider lives in a burrow in the ground. It makes a trap by spinning out long threads.

The wolf spider sits on a leaf, waiting for a small animal to pass by.

*This green lynx spider is
hiding inside the leaf of a
plant, ready to jump out.*

When an insect

stumbles over

the trap, the spider

leaps out and grabs it.

Centipedes are fast-running animals.

They catch wood lice, slugs, and insects.

*This centipede has
caught a cockroach
in its powerful jaws.*

Dangerous animals

Centipedes and spiders have jaws which inject a **poison** into the bodies of their prey. Sometimes, the poison kills the animal at once. Other poisons **paralyze** the

A funnel-web spider uses its jaws to inject a poison that can kill large animals.

animal. This means that the prey is still alive, but cannot move its body.

This wandering spider (above) has caught a small frog.

The bite of some spiders, such as the black widow, is so poisonous that it can kill a human.

You can see one of the large jaws of this centipede, between its head and its first leg.

Harmless animals

Millipedes are **herbivores**. This means that they eat only plants. They use their jaws to chew leaves or wood. You can often find them in rotting logs and under the bark of dead trees.

A giant millipede eats fallen leaves on the forest floor.

When a millipede is attacked, it protects itself by curling up into a coil.

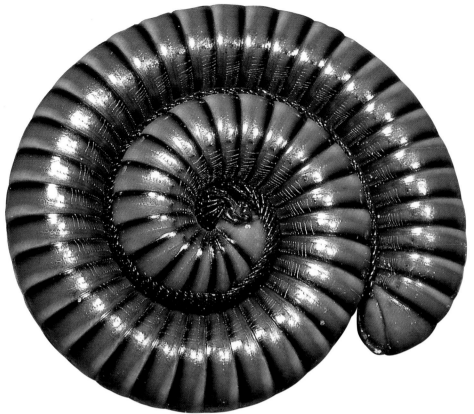

Some millipedes can squirt out a liquid that tastes nasty. The liquid puts off any animals that try to attack the millipede.

The body of a giant pill millipede is protected by heavy armor.

From egg to adult

A spider lays up to 800 eggs. The eggs are laid together in a ball. They are protected by a layer of yellow **silk**. After a few weeks, baby spiders hatch from the eggs. These tiny **spiderlings** grow quickly. They **shed** their skin to grow larger.

A female spider wraps up its eggs in silk.

Miniature spiders hatch from the eggs. They can be less than 1/4 inch (6 mm) long.

A centipede lays its eggs one at a time. Each egg is covered with a sticky liquid so that it sticks to the soil. Tiny baby centipedes hatch from the eggs.

A wolf spider carries its babies on its back for a few weeks after they hatch.

Watching minibeasts

You can find spiders almost anywhere, indoors and out. They are difficult to keep, so it is best to watch them in the wild. Try looking for a spider's web after rain or frost, when the silk threads shine with water. Draw the patterns of the webs you find. If you watch garden spiders closely, you may see them trap their prey. Centipedes and millipedes live under rotting logs and bark, and among dead leaves. A compost heap is a good place to look for them.

A damp, shady log pile is often home to spiders, centipedes, millipedes, and other minibeasts.

You can find lots of minibeasts among soil and dead leaves.

Ask an adult to help you collect some soil and dead leaves. Tip some out on to a large sheet of white paper. Use a magnifying glass to watch any minibeasts you find. The paper makes it easier to spot them as they run around. Make sure you return all the leaves and animals to the place you found them.

You may be able to buy large, hissing millipedes in a pet store. They are harmless, noisy animals which can be kept in an old fish tank.

Hissing millipedes like to eat lettuce leaves. Put a layer of soil, leaves, and twigs on the bottom of their tank.

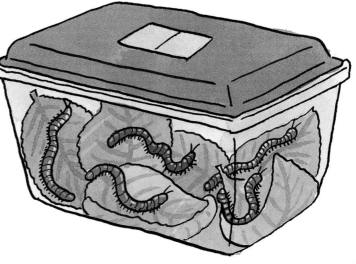

29

Minibeast sizes

Spiders, centipedes, and millipedes are many sizes. The pictures in this book do not show them at their actual size. Below you can see how big they are in real life.

Money spider
⅛ – ¼ inch long
(3–5 mm)

Common centipede
1¼ inches (30 mm) long

Calico spider
3½ inches long
(90 mm)

Tarantula
up to 6 inches (150 mm) long

Velvet mite
⅛ inch (3 mm) long

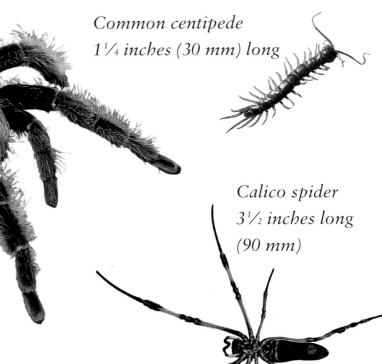

Glossary

abdomen The rear part of a spider's body.

arachnid An animal with eight legs, such as a spider.

armored Covered with a strong, hard case.

carnivore An animal that eats other animals.

herbivore An animal that eats only plants.

insect An animal with six legs and three parts to its body.

joint The place where two parts of a limb are joined. Limbs can bend at a joint.

paralyze To stop an animal from being able to move its muscles.

poison A harmful substance.

prey Animals that are killed by other animals for food.

segment One part of a body.

shed To get rid of something naturally, such as skin or hair.

silk Thin, strong threads made by a spider.

sting The part of an animal that squirts out poison.

spiderling A baby spider.

Index

U.S. publication copyright © 2000 Thameside Press.

International copyright reserved in all countries.
No part of this book may be reproduced in any form
without written permission from the publisher.

Distributed in the United States by
Smart Apple Media
1980 Lookout Drive
North Mankato, MN 56003

Text copyright © Sally Morgan 2000
Illustrations by Woody

Editor: Russell McLean
Designers: John Jamieson, Ian Butterworth
Picture researcher: Sally Morgan
Educational consultant: Emma Harvey

ISBN: 1-929298-82-X

Printed in the USA

9 8 7 6 5 4 3 2 1

Library of Congress Cataloging-in-Publication Data

Morgan, Sally.
    Spiders, centipedes, and millipedes / by Sally Morgan.
        p. cm. -- (Looking at minibeasts)
    Summary: Describes the physical characteristics and habits
of various kinds of spiders and of centipedes and millipedes.
    ISBN 1-929298-82-X
    1. Spiders--Juvenile literature. 2. Centipedes--Juvenile
literature. [1. Spiders. 2. Centipedes. 3. Millipedes.] I. Title.

QL458.4 .M64 2000
595.4'4--dc21   00-024748

Picture acknowledgements: W. Lawlor/Ecoscene: 15t.
Raymond Mendez/OSF: 21b. Sally Morgan/Ecoscene: 8, 30br.
Papilio: front & back cover tcr, 1, 4, 6, 9t, 9c, 14-15, 19br, 26,
30cl. Jean Preston-Mafham/Premaphotos: 21t. Ken Preston-
Mafham/Premaphotos: front cover tcl, tr, cl, b; back cover tcl
& tr, 3t, 3b, 5t, 7b, 11t, 12, 13t, 15c, 19tr, 22, 23t, 24, 25t,
25b, 27t, 30cr. Rod Preston-Mafham/Premaphotos: 23b, 27b.
Barrie Watts: front & back cover tl, 2, 11b, 13b, 16, 17t, 17b,
18-19, 20. Robin Williams/Ecoscene: 5b, 7t, 10, 30bl & tr.